WEST CHICAGO PUBLIC LIBRARY DISTRICT
3 6653 00120 0223

W9-BNO-374

Invertebrates

Centipedes, Millipedes, and Their Relatives

Myriapods

Beth Blaxland
for the Australian Museum

This edition first published in 2003 in the United States of America by Chelsea House Publishers, a subsidiary of Haights Cross Communications.

Chelsea House Publishers
1974 Sproul Road, Suite 400
Broomall, PA 19008-0914

The Chelsea House world wide web address is www.chelseahouse.com

Library of Congress Cataloging-in-Publication Data Applied for.
ISBN 0-7910-6995-8

First published in 2002 by
MACMILLAN EDUCATION AUSTRALIA PTY LTD
627 Chapel St, South Yarra, Australia, 3141

Edited by Anna Fern
Text design by Polar Design Pty Ltd
Cover design by Polar Design Pty Ltd
Illustrations by Peter Mather, Watershed Art and Design
Australian Museum Publishing Unit: Jenny Saunders and Kate Lowe
Australian Museum Series Editor: Deborah White
Australian Museum Scientific Adviser: Dr Greg Edgecombe

Printed in China

Acknowledgements
Cover photograph: Centipede, courtesy of Jiri Lochman/Lochman Transparencies.

C. Andrew Henley/Auscape, p. 30; David Knowles/Lochman Transparencies, pp. 17 (top), (bottom right), 22 (bottom), 27 (top); Densey Clyne/Auscape, p. 22, (top); Gonzalo Giribet/Nature Focus, pp. 15 (top), 24 (bottom), 25 (top); Gunther Schmida/ Lochman Transparencies, p. 11; Jean-Paul Ferrero/Auscape, pp. 5, 15 (bottom); Jiri Lochman/Lochman Transparencies, pp. 3, 4 (top), 6 (all), 7 (all), 8, 9, 13, 16 (middle), 18, 19, 20 (top), 24 (top), 25 (bottom), 26 (all), 27 (bottom); Kathie Atkinson/Auscape, pp. 11, 14, 23; Mark Newton/Auscape, pp. 20 (bottom), 29; Mike Gray/Nature Focus, p. 4 (bottom); Philip Griffin/Nature Focus, p. 28; Wayne Lawler/Auscape, p. 21.

Contents

Glossary words

When a word is printed in **bold**, you can look up its meaning in the Glossary on page 31.

What are myriapods?

Myriapods are a group of invertebrate animals. An invertebrate is an animal that does not have a backbone. There are many different kinds of invertebrates. Some other examples of invertebrates are butterflies, worms and prawns. Can you think of any other invertebrates?

There are different kinds of myriapods and most of them live on land. The two main kinds of myriapods are:

- centipedes
- millipedes.

Centipedes and millipedes are the myriapods that people see the most, but there are also two other kinds of myriapods. They are:

- pauropods
- symphylans.

These are very small myriapods that are almost always less than one-half inch (1 centimeter) long.

A millipede is a myriapod.

This tiny symphylan is a myriapod.

Fascinating fact

There are about 14,000 different types of myriapods. Most of these myriapods are centipedes and millipedes.

General features of myriapods

Myriapods' closest relatives are invertebrates such as **insects**, spiders and **crustaceans**. Insects, spiders, crustaceans and myriapods all belong to a big group of invertebrates called arthropods.

All adult arthropods, including myriapods, have the same general features. Arthropods are invertebrates that have:

- a stiff skeleton, called an exoskeleton, outside their body. This covers the body like hard skin and is shed from time to time as the arthropod grows.
- **limbs** with joints. These joints allow the limbs to bend.

Myriapods are a little different from other kinds of arthropods, such as insects, spiders and crustaceans. Myriapods are the only arthropods that have:

- a body made up of two parts: a head and a long trunk
- two **antennae** on their head that help them feel, smell and taste
- a trunk made up of many similar parts called **segments** (these segments look like rings around the body)
- 18 or more legs on their trunk.

Did you know

Myriapod means many feet. Myriapods were given this name because they have so many legs.

How do you say it?

antennae: *an-**ten**-ee*
arthropods: ***arth**-ro-pods*
centipedes: ***sent**-i-peeds*
crustaceans: *krus-**tay**-shuns*
invertebrate: *in-**vert**-a-bret*
millipedes: ***mill**-i-peeds*
myriapods: ***mir**-ee-uh-pods*
pauropods: ***pore**-o-pods*
symphylans: ***sim**-fy-lens*

A centipede is a myriapod.

Myriapod bodies

A myriapod's body has two parts: a head and a long trunk. Some myriapods have eyes on their heads, but some do not have eyes. The head has two antennae. The trunk is made up of many segments and many legs. An adult myriapod has 18 or more legs on its trunk and many myriapods have hundreds of legs. Each leg has joints and can bend. The head, trunk and legs are all covered by a stiff exoskeleton.

The bodies of the two main kinds of myriopods, centipedes and millipedes, look different from each other.

Centipedes

Centipedes have long, flat bodies. A centipede's trunk has many segments and almost all of the segments have two legs each. An adult centipede has 30 legs or more and these legs are quite long and thick. Most of its legs stick out on each side of its body. Its last two legs are very long and stick out backwards at the tail end of its body.

This is a centipede.

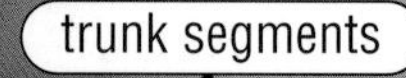

A centipede has two long antennae on the very front of its head. Under its head, there are two poison claws that the centipede uses to catch its food. These poison claws grow out of the first trunk segment. Each poison claw ends in a curved fang with a pointed tip.

Centipedes have long antennae. Most centipede trunk segments have two legs – one leg on each side of each segment.

Millipedes

Most millipedes have long bodies that are rounded on top and flat underneath. A millipede's trunk has many segments, and there are four legs on almost all of the segments. An adult millipede has 22 or more legs, and many have hundreds of legs. These legs are quite short and thin. They do not have legs that stick out at the tail end of their bodies like centipedes do, and they do not have poison claws. Millipedes have two antennae on their heads. These antennae can sometimes be hard to see because they are short and may be held close to the head.

head

This is a millipede. It has many short, thin legs under its body.

Did you know?

The bodies of most adult centipedes are less than 2.5 inches (6 centimeters) long, but some kinds of centipedes grow as long as 12 inches (30 centimeters).

Some adult millipedes are very tiny. Others grow to be 12 inches (30 centimeters) long.

Fascinating fact

Adult myriapods have between 18 and 750 legs.
Pauropods have 18 to 22 legs.
Symphylans have 24 legs.
Centipedes have 30 to 382 legs.
Millipedes have 22 to 750 legs.

Millipedes have short antennae. Most trunk segments have four legs – two legs on each side of each segment.

Special features of myriapod bodies

Exoskeleton

Like other arthropods, myriapods have a skeleton on the outside of their bodies. This skeleton covers the whole body like stiff, tough skin. It gives the body its shape and helps protect the body from damage. A skeleton that is found on the outside of an animal's body is called an exoskeleton.

Fascinating fact

When a myriapod molts, it replaces its old exoskeleton with a new, bigger one. At first, the new exoskeleton is soft, and the myriapod cannot move or eat. It can take a day or two for the new exoskeleton to become hard and stiff. When this happens, the myriapod can crawl about and feed.

Did you know ?

When a myriapod molts, its new exoskeleton is, at first, white or a pale color. The exoskeleton then changes color and becomes darker.

A myriapod has to **molt** its exoskeleton from time to time and grow a new, bigger exoskeleton. It has to do this because its stiff exoskeleton cannot stretch to fit its growing body. To grow into an adult, a myriapod has to molt many times.

A myriapod, such as this millipede, has a stiff exoskeleton covering its body.

Trunk segments

A myriapod's trunk is made up of many segments covered with a stiff exoskeleton. The exoskeleton is thinner between each of the trunk segments so that the myriapod's long body can bend. Most millipedes have many short segments that look the same along their trunk. Most centipedes have a mixture of long and short segments along their trunk.

Many legs with joints

Myriapods have many legs, and each leg has seven joints. These joints join two different parts of a leg so the leg can bend or twist. People also have joints in their hips, knees, ankles, toes and other parts of their bodies. Joints make it easier for us to move about.

Having joints in their legs allows myriapods to bend their legs. This makes it easier for them to move about. Myriapods bend their legs to crawl. Most millipedes have short legs and crawl slowly, but many centipedes have long legs and can crawl or run very quickly.

This picture shows some of a centipede's trunk segments and legs. Each of these legs is on a different trunk segment. The centipede can crawl because its legs have joints and can bend.

Did you know?

A centipede's legs are easy to see because they stick out from the sides of its body. A millipede's legs are often hard to see because they are under its body.

The life cycles of myriapods

Myriapods usually make new myriapods by sexual reproduction. The adult female provides eggs, and the adult male provides **sperm**. When an egg and a sperm join, a new myriapod begins to grow.

Myriapods have two main kinds of life cycle. In one life cycle, the young myriapods hatch with fully formed bodies and look like tiny adults. In the other life cycle, the young myriapods hatch with partly formed bodies and look different from the adults.

A life cycle where the young hatch with fully formed bodies

Some kinds of centipedes produce young that hatch with all their trunk segments and legs. These young centipedes look like tiny adults.

An adult male centipede often has special ways to introduce himself to an adult female before they **reproduce**. For example, the male may tap the tail end of the female with his antennae. Most males also build a web out of thin strands of silk they make in their bodies. The male places a bundle of his sperm on the web. The female then crawls across the web and picks up the sperm.

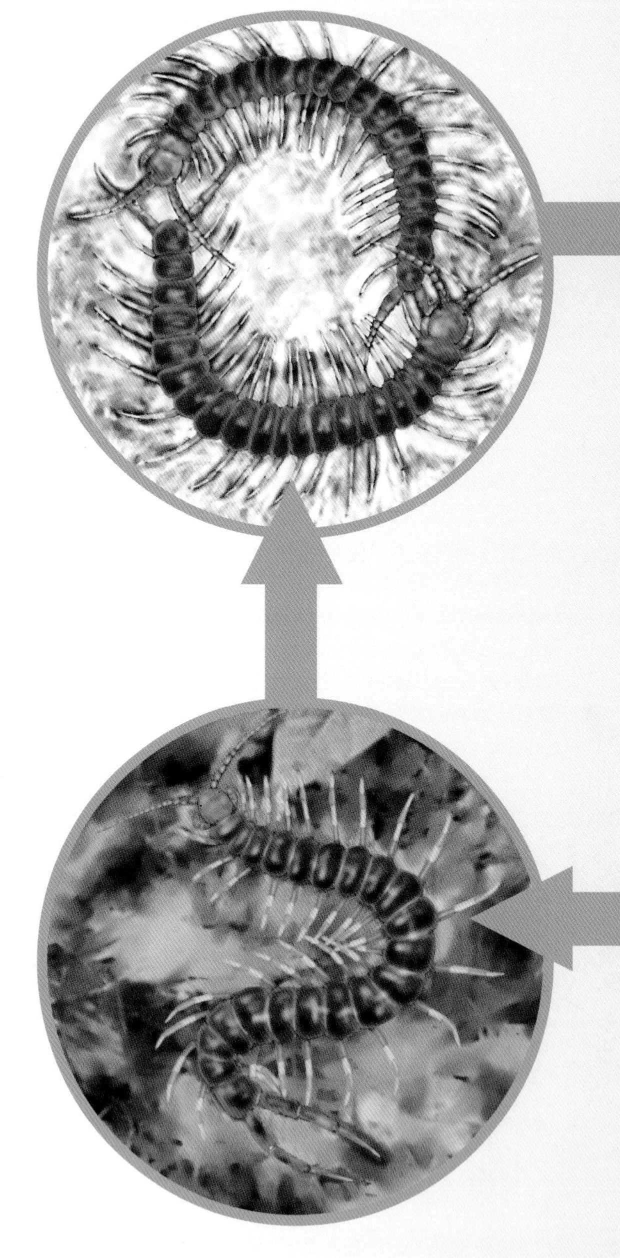

The young centipedes keep molting to grow bigger. They become adults in about one year. The adults are then ready to find a mate and reproduce.

When an egg and a sperm join, a young centipede begins to grow inside the egg. The female lays these eggs in the soil or under a rock or log. Then she curls around the eggs to look after them until they hatch.

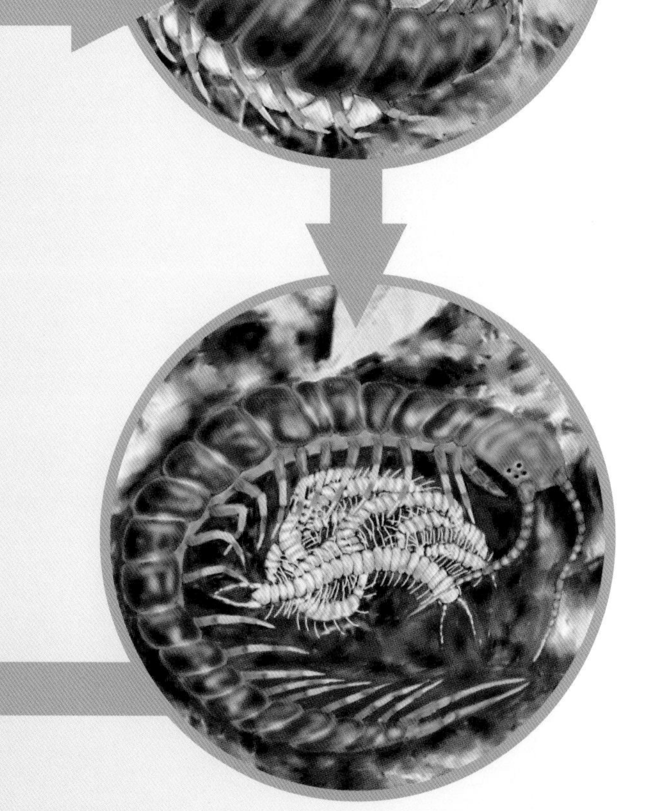

This centipede has laid her eggs under a log and then curled her body around the eggs to protect them.

These young centipedes are tiny, but they hatched with the same number of trunk segments and legs as their parents.

When the young centipedes hatch from their eggs, they look like tiny adults. These young centipedes have all their trunk segments, legs and other body parts, but they are not ready to move about and look after themselves. The mother stays with them to protect them while they molt their exoskeletons to grow a little bigger. After they have molted twice, they have grown into young centipedes that are big enough to leave their mother's care. If they do not leave now, the mother may eat them!

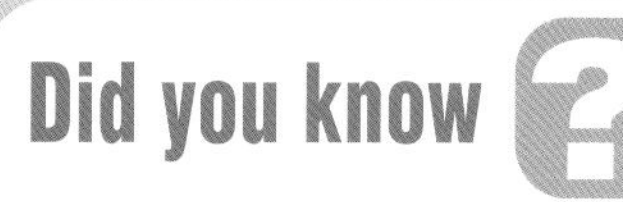

Most centipedes live for about three years, but some live for about six years.

A life cycle where the young hatch with partly formed bodies

Most myriapods produce young that hatch with bodies that are only partly formed. These young myriapods look different from the adults because they have not yet grown all their trunk segments and legs. Millipedes, pauropods, symphylans and some kinds of centipedes all have this kind of life cycle.

Male myriapods often have special ways to introduce themselves to a female. Some males tap their antennae on the female's back or legs. Some males climb onto the female's back.

To reproduce, an adult female provides eggs and an adult male provides sperm. Some male and female myriapods twist their bodies around each other. Then the male uses special legs on his body to place his sperm inside the female's body. Some male myriapods make a small web and then place a bundle of their sperm on the web for the female to pick up.

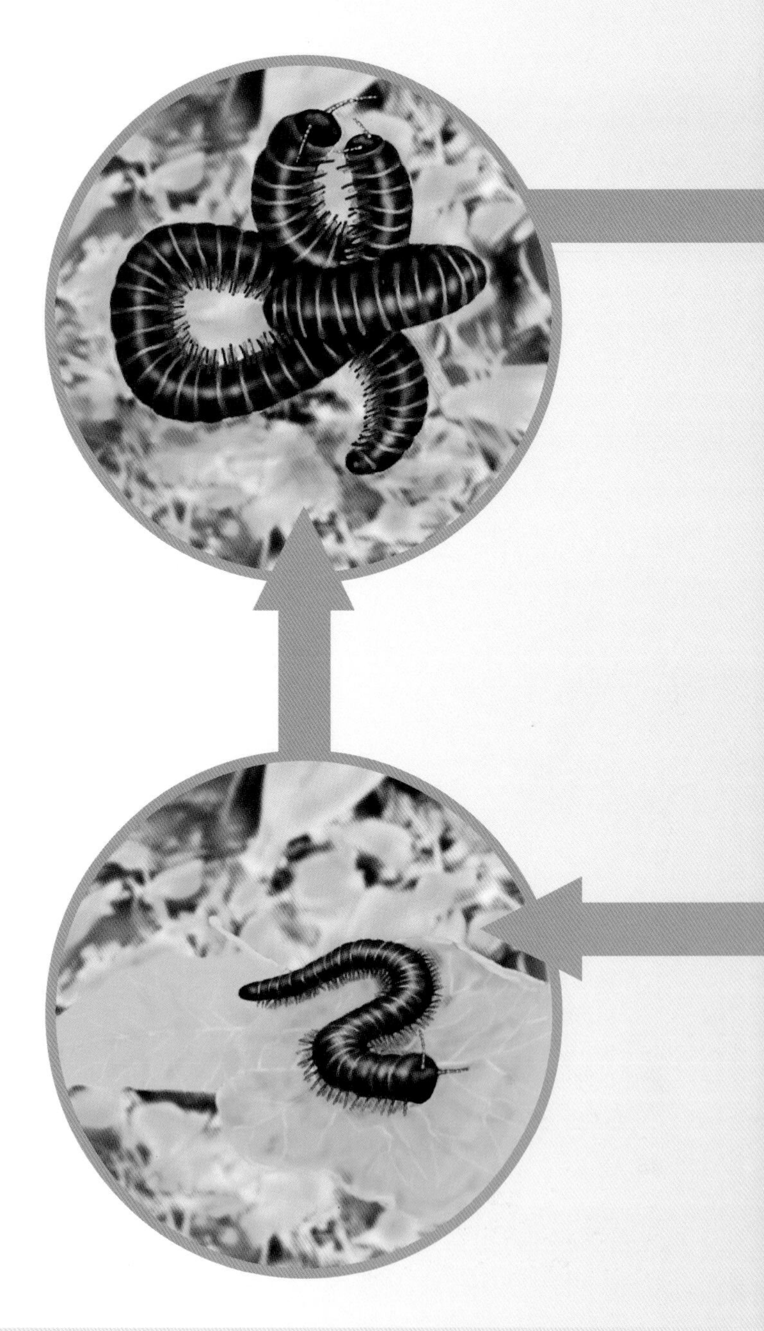

The young myriapods now have all their segments and legs and look like tiny adults. These young myriapods grow a little bigger each time they molt, and grow into adults when they are about one to two years old. The adult myriapods are then ready to reproduce.

When an egg and a sperm join, a young myriapod begins to grow inside the egg. The female lays these eggs in the soil or under leaves and twigs on the ground. Some females make a special cocoon or a nest to protect their eggs.

Most myriapods leave their eggs hidden on the ground, but some adult millipedes stay with their eggs. The female or male millipede curls around the egg nest to look after their eggs until they hatch.

Millipedes grow into adults when they are about one to two years old.

The eggs hatch after a few weeks to produce young myriapods called **larvae**. The larvae look different from the adults because they do not have as many trunk segments and legs as the adults. The larvae molt their exoskeletons many times. When they molt, they grow bigger and grow extra trunk segments and legs.

Fascinating fact

Adult millipedes have four legs on most of their trunk segments, but millipede larvae that have just hatched have only two legs on their trunk segments.

How do you say it?

larvae: ***lar**-vee*

Where myriapods live

Most myriapods live on land. They can be found all around the world, but they are more common in the **tropics**. They usually live in **habitats** on the ground or in the soil just below the surface of the ground.

On the ground

Most myriapods live on the ground. They usually stay in the shade away from the bright sun and find damp, dark places for shelter. Many myriapods live on the ground in forests. They can also be found in parks and gardens. They find shelter under the cover of dead leaves, twigs and bark lying on the ground. They also seek shelter in thick lawns.

Some myriapods look for shelter under stones and logs on the ground. They stay in these cool, dark and damp places during the day, but come out at night to look for food. Some kinds of centipedes are often found under stones. Their flat bodies can squeeze and bend to fit into small spaces under the stones.

Most myriapods, like this millipede, live on the ground.

In the soil

Some centipedes and millipedes burrow through the soil near the surface of the ground. Most of these myriapods are blind. Centipedes that burrow have long, thin bodies and can wiggle through loose soil like earthworms. Millipedes that burrow often have pointed heads. They use their strong legs and pointed heads to push their bodies through the soil like little bulldozers.

Fascinating fact

Many millipedes that live near the Amazon River in South America can climb trees. These millipedes live in the treetops when the river floods the ground.

This is a blind centipede that burrows through the soil.

Other habitats

Centipedes and millipedes live in a variety of other habitats. Some live inside caves and some live on the seashore. Myriapods that live on the seashore seek shelter under stones, shells and seaweeds that have washed up.

Sometimes millipedes and centipedes can be found inside damp buildings. There is even one kind of centipede called a house centipede. House centipedes are sometimes found inside damp bathrooms, laundry rooms or cellars, but their natural habitat is outside under logs and stones or in narrow cracks in rocks or the ground.

Did you know?

If a centipede or millipede wanders into a house, it needs to find a damp place to live. Otherwise its body will dry out and it will die.

Some myriapods, such as this centipede, live inside caves.

How myriapods sense the world

Myriapods have different senses to find out about the world around them. These senses let myriapods know if there is danger nearby and where to find food and shelter. Many myriapods have eyes. All myriapods have antennae, which are used to feel, taste and smell things. Myriapods also sense things with other parts of their bodies.

Light

Many centipedes and millipedes have eyes on their heads. A myriapod's eyes can sense if its surroundings are light or dark, but cannot see colors or shapes. Many myriapods use this sense to find dark places for shelter, such as under stones or piles of leaves. Most myriapods have tiny eyes, and a **microscope** is sometimes needed to see them. Some myriapods have only two tiny eyes. Others have a group of tiny eyes or eye lenses on each side of their head.

This centipede has four tiny eyes on each side of its head.

Did you know 

Some millipedes are attracted to light. When they sense light, they crawl towards it. These millipedes can sometimes be a pest in people's houses because they crawl towards house lights at night and then crawl inside.

Some myriapods do not have eyes. Many of these myriapods can still sense if it is light or dark because their body surface can sense light. This is useful for myriapods that burrow in the soil, as they can use this sense to help them stay underground where it is dark.

Touch

All myriapods have the sense of touch. Myriapods have tiny hairs on their bodies that help them sense when something touches them. These hairs stick out of their exoskeleton and are so tiny that a microscope is needed to see them. Myriapods have a lot of these tiny hairs on their antennae. This means their antennae are very good at feeling things. Many centipedes also use their long back legs to feel things behind them.

This centipede uses its long antennae to feel things in front of its body. It also uses its long back legs to feel things behind its body.

Smell and taste

A myriapod's antennae can smell and taste chemicals in its surroundings. When a myriapod moves about, it waves its antennae about in the air and keeps touching things. This helps it smell and taste its surroundings. Some myriapods can also taste things with special parts on the sides of their mouths.

Millipedes have short antennae to smell, taste and feel. If you look closely at this millipede's antennae, you will see some of the tiny hairs that help it sense things in its surroundings.

This centipede is waving its long antennae to smell the air.

Fascinating fact

Myriapods sense many things with their antennae, so it is important for them to keep their antennae clean. Myriapods spend a lot of time cleaning their antennae by wiping them with their mouths or front legs.

What myriapods eat

Centipedes mostly catch other small animals to feed on. Millipedes mostly eat dead and rotting plants, but some eat living plants and some eat other invertebrate animals.

Did you know 

Centipedes find their prey using their senses of touch and smell. They wave their antennae about to feel and smell their surroundings and they also feel for prey with their two very long back legs that stick out behind their body.

Centipedes

Most centipedes eat other animals. They eat invertebrates such as insects, spiders, earthworms, snails and millipedes. Certain large centipedes also eat some **vertebrates**, such as small frogs, lizards, snakes, birds and mice.

Fascinating fact

Some centipedes are very fast and can catch flying insects such as flies, bees and wasps. To catch a flying insect, a centipede quickly lifts up the front part of its body and grabs the insect out of the air as it flies past.

These centipedes are **predators**. They get their food by hunting and killing other animals. When a centipede finds an animal to eat, it grabs hold of the animal with its poison claws or legs. Some centipedes even find and catch their **prey** with their long pincer-like legs at the tail-end of their body. When it has caught its prey, the centipede quickly stabs the animal with its poison claws and injects its poison. The centipede then holds its prey and bites off pieces to chew.

This centipede has caught a fly to eat. It is holding the fly with its poison claws.

This millipede is eating rotting wood.

Millipedes

Most millipedes eat plants or **detritus**. Detritus is made up of plants and animals that are rotting away. When plants and animals rot, they break up into smaller and smaller pieces and mix in with the soil. Most of the detritus that millipedes eat comes from rotting wood and leaves. Some millipedes eat detritus as they burrow through the soil. Others find rotting leaves or logs to eat on the ground.

Fascinating fact

Millipedes are very useful animals in the environment. They help to recycle dead plants into fertilizers in the soil. These fertilizers help living plants grow. Earthworms are also useful in this way, but, in some places in the tropics, millipedes are better at this job than earthworms.

How do you say it?

detritus: *de-**try**-tus*
prey: *pray*

Some millipedes eat other kinds of food. Some chew on living plants, including roots and fruits that grow on the ground such as young melons. Some millipedes have long pointed beaks that they stab into plants to suck out the plant's sap. Some millipedes eat other invertebrates such as snails, earthworms and insects.

How myriapods defend themselves

Myriapods have many ways to defend themselves. Centipedes are often fast enough to escape danger, but they are also good at hiding. If a predator gets too close, centipedes can attack with their poison claws or their long back legs. Millipedes are good at hiding. They also have hard exoskeletons and harmful chemicals in their bodies to protect them.

Escaping

Most centipedes have long legs and can quickly run from danger. Some centipedes can even break off or shed some of their legs if a predator catches hold of them. When a centipede sheds some of its legs, it still has plenty of other legs to run away. The missing legs grow back the next time the centipede molts.

This centipede has tried to hide but has been caught by a predator.

Fascinating fact

One kind of centipede from Africa has an interesting way of escaping predators. Each of its back legs is big, flat and leaf-like. When it sheds one of these legs, the leg shakes for quite a while. This can distract the predator and help the centipede escape.

Hiding

Centipedes and millipedes are very good at hiding under stones, logs, leaves, bark or in burrows in the ground. Most centipedes and millipedes hide during the day and only come out at night when it is harder for predators to see them. Some centipedes have colors and patterns that make them hard to see in their surroundings. This **camouflage** helps these myriapods hide from predators.

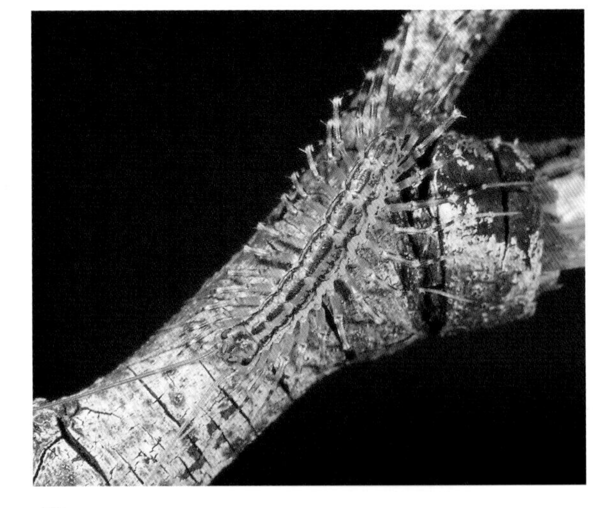

The colors and patterns on this centipede's body help camouflage it.

When millipedes are disturbed, they often curl up into a spiral with their head in the middle.

Exoskeleton

A millipede's exoskeleton is very thick and hard on the top and sides of its body. This means the top and sides of the body are well protected. The underparts are not as well protected because the exoskeleton is thinner and softer underneath the body where the legs are.

To protect their softer underparts, most millipedes can roll their bodies up into a spiral. Some can roll into a ball. When they do this, the hard parts of their exoskeleton cover up their soft underparts and protect them. They also curl up with their head in the middle of the spiral or ball. This protects their antennae and the rest of their head from damage.

How do you say it?

camouflage: ***kam**-uh-flaj*

Fascinating fact

Myriapods hide when they molt because their bodies are not protected when they shed their tough exoskeleton. Some myriapods hide in the soil or under leaves, stones or logs on the ground. Many millipedes build a special shelter to hide in when they molt. This shelter is made out of soil mixed with the millipede's droppings.

Poison claws

Only centipedes have poison claws. Centipedes use their poison claws to catch and kill their food and to defend themselves. Each poison claw ends in a pointed fang. Centipedes defend themselves by biting predators and injecting their poison. A bite can be very painful and can even kill some small animals.

Fascinating fact

A centipede's poison claws are not part of its mouth or head. They are special legs on the front of the centipede's trunk. These legs are not used for moving about. Instead, they are fangs for catching food.

This centipede has been turned over so you can see the two big poison claws under its head. Joints allow the centipede to open and close its poison claws when it attacks.

Pinching

Some kinds of centipedes defend themselves with the two long legs that stick out behind their bodies. These special legs are not used for crawling about. Instead, they help a centipede grab hold of prey, mate, and defend itself. Each of these special legs has a small claw on the end and many small spines underneath. When the centipede is attacked, it can strike out with these legs to grasp and pinch the attacker's skin.

These are the long legs on the tail end of a centipede's body. These legs can hold on to an animal while the centipede quickly twists around to bite with its front end.

Producing nasty chemicals

Centipedes and millipedes produce a variety of chemicals to defend themselves. Some of these chemicals smell horrible, some taste horrible, some are poisonous, some are sticky and some even make a predator go to sleep.

Centipedes

Some of the chemicals centipedes produce smell or taste horrible and make predators leave them alone. Some centipedes produce a sticky liquid. This liquid is often used on ants that attack centipedes. This chemical makes the ants so sticky they cannot move. Some centipedes produce chemicals that burn or cause itching.

Millipedes

Most millipedes produce chemicals. Often these chemicals ooze out from tiny holes in the sides of their trunk segments, but some millipedes in the tropics can squirt their chemicals as far as 20 inches (50 centimeters). The chemicals produced by millipedes can keep away ants, spiders, frogs, lizards, birds and many other animals.

Different millipedes produce different chemicals. Some produce a yellow, brown or white liquid and some produce a gas. One kind of millipede in Europe produces a chemical that stops spiders from attacking them by making the spiders go to sleep.

Did you know ?

Millipedes cannot bite or sting, but some of them make chemicals that can stain a person's skin or even make the skin red and produce blisters.

Most millipedes defend themselves with chemicals they release from tiny holes in their exoskeleton. If you look closely, you will see these tiny holes along the sides of this millipede's body.

up close

The different

There are thousands of different kinds of centipedes in the world, but scientists divide them into five main groups. Each group has centipedes with different body features.

House centipedes

House centipedes have 30 very long legs. They grow up to 2.75 inches (7 centimeters) long and their bodies are not as flat as the bodies of other centipedes. A house centipede's antennae are very long, thin and whip-like. Just behind their antennae are two big eyes. These eyes are bigger than other centipedes' eyes.

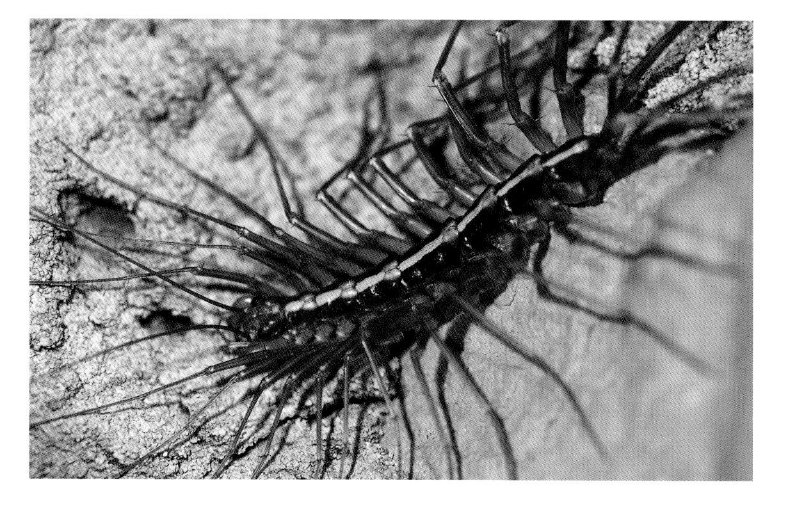

This is a house centipede.

Stone centipedes

Stone centipedes also have 30 legs, but they have a different body shape from house centipedes. Stone centipedes have flat bodies. Some grow as long as 1.5 inches (4 centimeters), but most are smaller.

Fascinating fact

The word centipede means "100 feet," but most centipedes have a lot fewer. The only centipedes that have as many as 100 feet are some of the longer earth centipedes.

This is a stone centipede.

groups of centipedes

Earth centipedes

Some earth centipedes grow about 6.5 inches (17 centimeters) long, but most are much shorter. They have a long, slender body and short legs. These centipedes have between 54 and 382 legs. They do not have eyes.

This is an earth centipede.

This is a scolopendrid centipede.

Scolopendrid centipedes

Scolopendrid centipedes have either 42 or 46 legs. Their bodies are flattened and quite wide. Most of these centipedes are less than 4 inches (10 centimeters) long, but some giant ones grow as long as 12 inches (30 centimeters). These centipedes often have colorful bodies and may be red, pink, yellow, orange, green, blue or a mixture of colors.

Craterostigmus centipedes

Craterostigmus centipedes are found only in Australia and New Zealand. In Australia, these centipedes live in moist forests in Tasmania. In New Zealand, they are mostly found on the South Island. They grow up to 2 inches (5 centimeters) long and have 30 legs. They also have long poison claws that stick out past the front of their heads.

Did you know

The biggest centipede in the world is a scolopendrid centipede. This giant centipede comes from certain parts of South America in the tropics.

How do you say it?

craterostigmus: ***krat**-ero-**stig**-mus*
scolopendrid: ***skol**-o-**pen**-drid*

up close Three different

There are many thousands of millipedes in the world. Different kinds of millipedes have different body features. Some millipedes have more trunk segments and legs than others. Some have a rounded body shape and others are more flattened.

There are so many different kinds of millipedes that scientists divide them into 15 different groups. Three of these groups are the pill millipedes, flat-backed millipedes and spirobolid millipedes.

This is a pill millipede.

Pill millipedes

Most millipedes have long, narrow bodies, but pill millipedes have short, wide bodies. They defend themselves by rolling up into a ball rather than rolling into a spiral like many other millipedes. Pill millipedes can grow up to 1.5 inches (4 centimeters) long. They have 12 or 13 trunk segments and 42 legs. They also have large eyes.

Pill millipedes can roll up into a ball.

Fascinating fact

Another kind of invertebrate can also roll up into a ball and looks a lot like a pill millipede. Some people call it a pill bug. It is also known as a wood louse, slater or sow bug. Pill bugs are crustaceans. They are smaller than pill millipedes and only have 14 walking legs.

How do you say it?

spirobolid: *spy-rob-ol-id*

groups of millipedes

Flat-backed millipedes

Many flat-backed millipedes are less than 2 inches (5 centimeters) long, but some grow over 6 inches (15 centimeters) long. These millipedes have a narrow body with 19 or 20 trunk segments and as many as 66 legs. They do not have eyes. Flat-backed millipedes often have a bulge on each side of their trunk segments. Sometimes these bulges are big and wing-like and this gives these millipedes a flattened appearance. This is why they are called flat-backed millipedes.

This is a flat-backed millipede.

Spirobolid millipedes

Some spirobolid millipedes grow as long as 8 inches (20 centimeters) and their body shape is long and narrow. Their long bodies are smooth and rounded. They have 35 to 60 trunk segments and more than 100 legs. Their many legs help them push their bodies through soil and piles of rotting leaves on the ground. These millipedes have tiny eyes.

Did you know 

Some millipedes are very colorful. For example, some flat-backed millipedes have red, orange, blue or purple spots or stripes.

Fascinating fact

The word millipede means "1,000 feet," but no millipede has this many feet.

This is a spirobolid millipede.

Where can you see myriapods?

Bushland habitats

Centipedes can often be found in natural woodlands, forests, grasslands and even in deserts. Millipedes are mostly found in moist forests such as rainforests. The best time to see myriapods is when it is not too hot and dry, and not too cold. They prefer to come out and move around at night, but you can often find these myriapods in cool, damp places during the day. Places where you might find centipedes and millipedes are under stones, logs or leaves on the ground and under loose bark on tree trunks.

If you find a myriapod, look at its body features and how it moves. Does it have a body that is rounded like an earthworm or does it have a flattened body? Can you see its trunk segments? Can you see if there are four legs on most trunk segments or if there are only two legs on a segment? Does it roll up when it is disturbed? Does it crawl slowly or does it run quickly? Is it a centipede or a millipede?

Most myriapods are seen on the ground under bark, logs, stones or other kinds of cover.

Gardens

Myriapods can sometimes be seen in flower gardens, vegetable gardens and lawns. They live in places where they can find shelter and plenty of food. Places to look for millipedes and centipedes include compost heaps and under piles of old leaves. These places provide dark, damp habitats to hide in during the day. They also provide food. Centipedes eat other invertebrates living in compost and piles of leaves. Millipedes eat rotting compost and leaves.

If you scratch down below the surface of a compost heap or a pile of old leaves, you may see a variety of invertebrates. Some of them may be centipedes or millipedes. When disturbed, the millipedes will either curl up into a ball or spiral, or they will slowly crawl away to look for somewhere dark to hide. The centipedes will quickly run away to hide.

Most myriapods come out at night to look for food on the ground. Some also climb and may be found on tree trunks or branches. During the day, they may be found under loose tree bark.

Safety tips

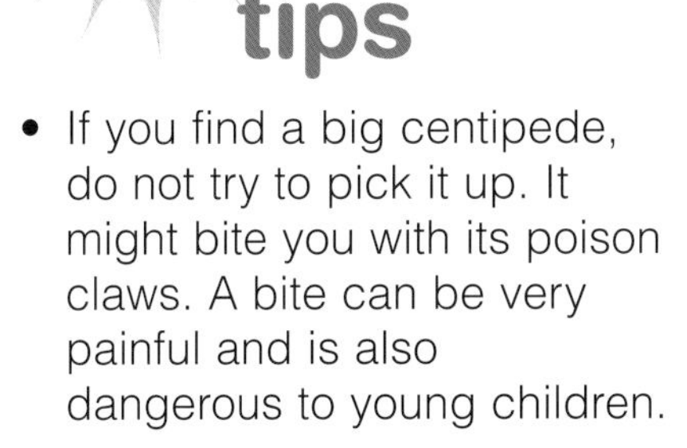

- If you find a big centipede, do not try to pick it up. It might bite you with its poison claws. A bite can be very painful and is also dangerous to young children.
- Most millipedes are harmless to people. If you find one, it is best not to pick it up, as many produce chemicals that can stain the skin.
- Big millipedes from the tropics should not be picked up, as some produce chemicals that can cause blisters on the skin.

Quiz

1. Is a myriapod an invertebrate? Why?
2. A myriapod's trunk is made up of many similar parts that look like rings around its body. What are these similar parts called?
3. Which kind of myriapod has poison claws?
4. Which kind of myriapod has four legs on most of its trunk segments?
5. What is an exoskeleton?
6. Do myriapod larvae look like their parents?
7. Do centipedes eat detritus?
8. Where does a millipede put its head when it rolls its body into a spiral?
9. Can millipedes bite or sting?
10. Does a house centipede have very long legs or very short legs?

Turn to page 32 to check your answers.

Challenge QUESTIONS

1. Why do myriapods need to molt?
2. Why do myriapods spend a lot of time cleaning their antennae?
3. Why do myriapods need to hide when they molt?
4. Some myriapods have poison claws. Do these poison claws join onto the head or onto the trunk?
5. A pill bug has 14 walking legs. Does this make it a myriapod, or is it a different kind of invertebrate? Why?

Some centipede bodies have interesting colors on them.

Glossary

antennae Long hair-like or short, spiky stalks on the heads of myriapods, crustaceans and insects. Antennae are used to feel, smell and taste things.

camouflage Colors, patterns and ways of covering an animal's body that make the animal hard to see against its background.

crustaceans A group of invertebrate animals that includes crayfishes, crabs, shrimps, prawns and pill bugs. A crustacean has a body covered by a hard skeleton, legs with joints and four antennae on its head.

detritus Food made up of plants and animals that have rotted away into tiny pieces.

habitats The places where living things, such as plants and animals, live.

insects A group of invertebrate animals that includes flies, ants, beetles and butterflies. An adult insect has a body covered by a stiff skeleton, two antennae on its head and six legs with joints.

larvae Young myriapods that look very different from adults.

limbs Body parts that branch off from the main part of an animal's body. These body parts can be leg-like, arm-like or pincer-like and help an animal eat and move about.

microscope A special magnifying glass used by scientists to see very tiny things.

molt When a myriapod or another kind of arthropod sheds its stiff exoskeleton so it can grow bigger.

predators Animals that hunt other animals to eat.

prey Animals that are eaten by other animals.

reproduce To make more of the same kind of animal or plant.

segments Parts of the body that have a similar structure. A myriapod's body has a trunk made up of many segments. Each segment often looks like a ring around the myriapod's body.

sperm Cells from a male animal's body that can fertilize the eggs from a female animal's body to reproduce.

tropics The part of Earth between the Tropic of Cancer and the Tropic of Capricorn, where air and water temperatures are always warm or hot.

vertebrates Animals that have a backbone.

Index

Answers to quiz

1. Yes, because a myriapod is an animal that does not have a backbone.
2. Segments.
3. A centipede.
4. A millipede.
5. A skeleton that is found on the outside of an animal's body.
6. No, myriapod larvae look very different from their parents.
7. No (most centipedes eat other animals; millipedes eat detritus).
8. In the middle of the spiral.
9. No.
10. Very long legs.

Answers to challenge questions

1. They need to molt so they can grow bigger. (Their stiff exoskeletons cannot stretch to fit their growing bodies, so they need to replace their old exoskeleton with a new, bigger one.)
2. Myriapods sense many things with their antennae (including touch, smells and tastes) and they would not be able to sense these things properly with dirty antennae.
3. Myriapods' bodies are not protected when they shed their tough exoskeleton because their new exoskeleton is soft. (This means they have to hide from predators until their new exoskeleton hardens.)
4. The trunk.
5. A pill bug is not a myriapod because all myriapods have 18 or more legs. (A pill bug is a crustacean.)